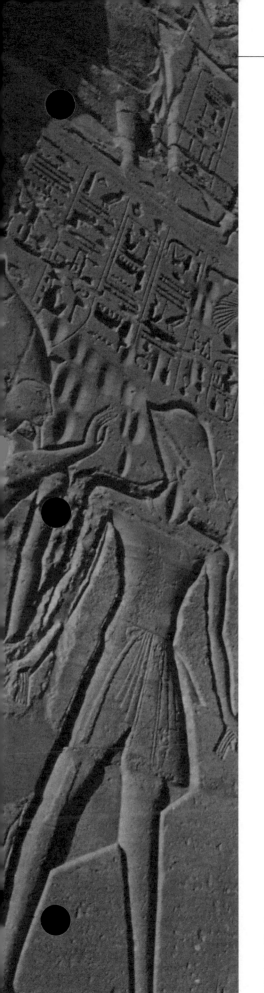

History Alive!®
The Ancient World

This book of visuals is provided for use with classroom digital devices.
Digital versions of these visuals are available with the purchase of a
History Alive! The Ancient World TeachTCI subscription. Overhead
transparencies of these visuals are available for purchase on our
Web site, www.teachtci.com.

Chief Executive Officer: Bert Bower

Chief Operating Officer: Amy Larson

Director of Curriculum: Liz Russell

Managing Editor: Laura Alavosus

Editorial Project Manager: Nancy Rogier

Project Editor: Pat Sills

Copyeditor: Susan Arnold

Editorial Associates: Anna Embree, Sarah Sudano

Production Manager: Lynn Sanchez

Art Director: John F. Kelly

Senior Graphic Designer: Christy Uyeno

Graphic Designers: Sarah Wildfang, Don Taka, Victoria Philp

Photo Edit Manager: Margee Robinson

Photo Editor: Diane Austin

Production Project Manager: Eric Houts

Art Editor: Mary Swab

Audio Director: Katy Haun

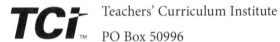

Teachers' Curriculum Institute

PO Box 50996

Palo Alto, CA 94303

Customer Service: 800-497-6138

www.teachtci.com

ISBN 978-1-58371-911-4

1 2 3 4 5 6 7 8 9 10 -WP- 14 13 12 11 10

Manufactured by Walsworth Publishing Company, Marceline, MO

United States of America, July 2010, 0-37305-0

NSF-SFI-COC-C0004285

Program Director

Bert Bower

Program Author

Wendy Frey

Creative Development Manager

Kelly Shafsky

Contributing Writers

John Bergez

Mark Falstein

Diane Hart

Marisa A. Howard

Amy Joseph

Curriculum Developers

Joyce Bartky

April Bennett

Nicole Boylan

Terry Coburn

Julie Cremin

Erin Fry

Amy George

Anne Maloney

Steve Seely

Nathan Wellborne

Reading Specialist

Kate Kinsella, Ed.D.
Reading and TESOL Specialist
San Francisco State University

Teacher Consultants

Melissa Aubuchon
Indian Trail Middle School
Plainfield, Illinois

Anthony Braxton
Cruickshank Middle School
Merced, California

Amy George
Weston Middle School
Weston, Massachusetts

Randi Gibson
Stanford Middle School
Long Beach, California

Lisa Macurak
New Windsor Middle School
New Windsor, Maryland

Sherry Owens
Lubbock Independent School District
Lubbock, Texas

Acknowledgments

Scholars

Dr. Anthony Bulloch
University of California, Berkeley

Dr. Mark W. Chavalas
*University of Wisconsin,
La Crosse*

Dr. Eun Mi Cho
*California State University
Sacramento*

Dr. Steve Farmer
Palo Alto, California

Dr. Bruce Grelle
California State University Chico

Dr. David N. Keightley
University of California, Berkeley

Dr. Brij Khare
*California State University
San Bernardino*

Dr. Gary Miles
*University of California,
Santa Cruz*

Dr. Daniel Veidlinger
California State University Chico

Dr. Jed Wyrick
California State University Chico

Dr. Joel Zimbelman
California State University Chico

Assessment Consultants

Denny Chandler
*Curriculum and Assessment
Specialist
Cold Spring, Kentucky*

Julie Weiss
*Curriculum and Assessment
Specialist
Elliot, Maine*

Assessment Consultants

Melanie Pinkert
*Music Faculty
Montgomery College, Maryland*

Cartographer

Mapping Specialists
Madison, Wisconsin

Internet Consultant

Amy George
Weston, Massachusetts

Diverse Needs Consultants

Erin Fry
Glendora, California

Colleen Guccione
Naperville, Illinois

Cathy Hix
*Swanson Middle School
Arlington, Virginia*

Photographs

Cover: Ian Mckinnell/Getty Images

Title page: Ian Mckinnell/Getty Images

1: Charles & Josette Lenars/Corbis 2: John Reader/National Geographic Image Collection 3: Robert Harding 4: Robert Harding 5: Robert Harding 6: Jack Unruh/National Geographic Image Collection 8: Sylvia Schofield/ Robert Harding 9: RF/Tfcannon/ Dreamstime.com 10: © V. Southwell/ Hutchison Picture Library 11: Gianni Dagli Orti/CORBIS 15: RF/Raymond Kasprzak/Shutterstock 16: © Richard T. Nowitz/CORBIS 17: © Royalty-Free/ CORBIS 18: RF/Mike P Shepherd / Alamy 19: RF/National Geographic/ SuperStock 21: RF/Al Franklin/Corbis 22: Werner Forman/Art Resource, NY 23: © Gianni Dagli Orti CORBIS 24: RF/20207851/Shutterstock 25: © Erich Lessing/Art Resource, NY 26: © Erich Lessing/Art Resource, NY 27: © Trustees of The British Museum 28: © Lloyd Townsend/National Geographic Image Collection 29: © Lloyd K. Townsend/National Geographic Image Collection 30: © David Blossom/ National Geograhic Image Collection 31: Robert Harding 32: Robert Harding 33: R & S Michaud/Woodfin Camp & Assoc. 34: © Andrea Pistolesi-The Image Bank/Getty Images 35: Robert Harding 36: Robert Harding 37: © John Elk III 38: © Carlos Freire/Hutchison Picture Library 40: HarappaBazzar 41: Robert Harding 42: Victoria & Albert Museum, London/Art Resource, NY 43: The Bhaktivedanta Book Trust International, © 1972. 44: The Bhaktivedanta Book Trust International, © 1972. 45: The Bhaktivedanta Book Trust International, © 1972. 47: By permission of The British Library, London 48: By permission of The British Library, London 49: By permission of The British Library, London 50: By permission of The British Library, London 51: By permission of The British Library, Londo 52: © Réunion des Musées Nationaux/Art Resource, NY 54: TCI 55: © Liu Lingcang/ChinaStock 56TL: Ronald Sherida/Ancient Art and Architecture Collection. 56BR: ©ChinaStock 56TR: © ChinaStock 56BL: © Wang Lu/ChinaStock 57: © Hsien-Min Yang/National Geographic Image Collection 58: Xinhua/Sovfoto 60: Giraudon/Art Resource, NY 61: Xinhua/Sovoto 62: The Art Archive 63: © Bettmann/CORBIS 64: © Royalty-Free/CORBIS 65: Science & Society Picture Library 68BL: Bogdan Giusca/Multi-license with GFDL and Creative Commons/Wikipedia 68BR: © James Davis; Eye Ubiquitous/ CORBIS 70B: North Wind Picture Archives 70T: North Wind Picture Archives 71: RF/Superstock 72: North Wind Picture Archives 73: ©RF/Ivy Close Images/Alamy 74: © Bettmann/ CORBIS 75: Bettmann/CORBIS 77: © Erich Lessing/Art Resource, NY 78: © Trustees of The British Museum 79: Bridgeman Art Library 80: © Copyright The British Museum 81B: The Granger Collection, New York 81T: North Wind Picture Archives 82: © Bettmann/CORBIS 83: North Wind Picture Archives 84: North Wind Picture Archives 85: RF/Clara/ Shutterstock 86: © Scala/ Art Resource, NY 87: North Wind Picture Archives 88: The Granger Collection, New York 89T: RF/Alamy 89M: © Pontino/Alamy 89B: © Eitan Simanor /Alamy 90T: RF/Fotosearch 90TR: © Blend Images/ Alamy 90BL: © RF/Radius Images/ Alamy 90BLLR: © M.T.M. Images/ Alamy 90BRU: © Steve Skjold/Alamy 90BLR: © Allen T. Jules/CORBIS 91: © ALANAH TORRALBA/epa/Corbis

Art

Chapter 3
7: Doug Roy

Chapter 7:
7A: Doug Roy

Chapter 8:
8F: DJ Simison

Chapter 20
20: Len Ebert

Cave Painting of a Human

Rock Painting

Homo Habilis

Homo Erectus

Homo Sapiens Neanderthalensis

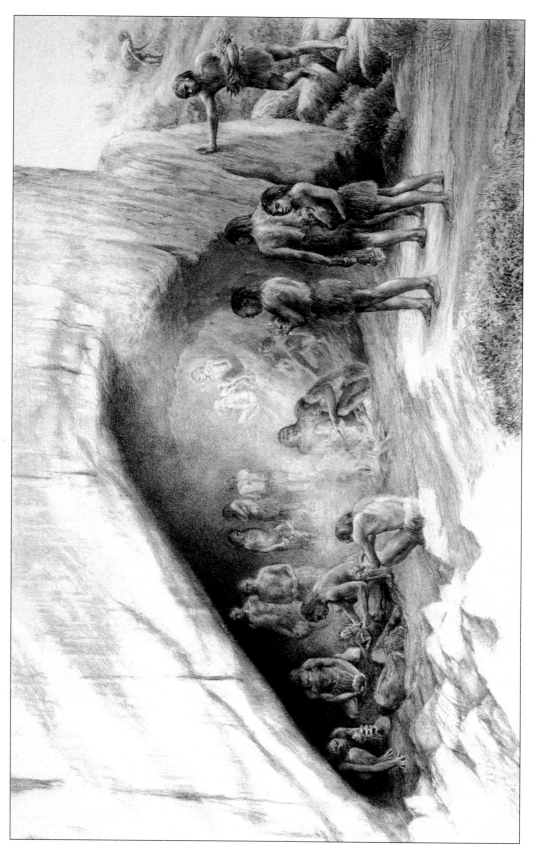

Homo Sapiens Sapiens

Sample Comic-Book Story Page

Back in Paleolithic times, people had to go from place to place to find their food. They hunted wild animals and gathered fruits, seeds, and grains from wild plants.

But in Neolithic times, . . .

You won't find me traveling around looking for wild plants to eat. Nowadays, we grow our own food by collecting and planting the seeds of different plants.

Hunting animals? I only do that on the weekends for fun! Now that we have learned how to domesticate animals, I spend my time herding our cows and goats, instead of battling bears and bison.

These changes are important because . . .

We eat better now, and we have a more stable food supply.

And we don't have to move around a lot looking for food. Want to join us for dinner?

Zagros Mountains

Problem A: You are a Mesopotamian living in one of the villages in the foothills. You must decide what to do about the food shortages in your village. Which of the following responses do you think will best address the problem?

A. Increase the number of times each year that farmers plant their crops.
B. Move down to the river plains and try to grow crops there.
C. Abandon farming and return to hunting and gathering.
D. Attack neighboring villages and steal their food.

Euphrates River

Problem B: You live in one of the villages on the Mesopotamian plains. To provide your village with a year-round supply of water, you must design a water-control system. Draw and label the best plan for this system. Your plan should include rivers and fields.

Irrigation Canal near the Euphrates River

Problem C: You live in one of the villages on the Mesopotamian plains. You must decide on the best way to maintain a complex irrigation system. Which of the following responses do you think will best address this problem?

A. Maintain only the canals around your village's fields.
B. Force members of another village to maintain the entire irrigation system throughout the year.
C. Cooperate with other villages to regularly maintain the entire irrigation system.
D. Abandon irrigation and return to collecting and carrying water from the river to the fields.

An Attacking Army

Problem D: You live in a Sumerian city. Neighboring communities are planning attacks on your city. You must design and draw a defense plan to protect the city. Make a simple drawing of the city, and design your plan around it.

A Landscape

Physical Features of Egypt and Kush

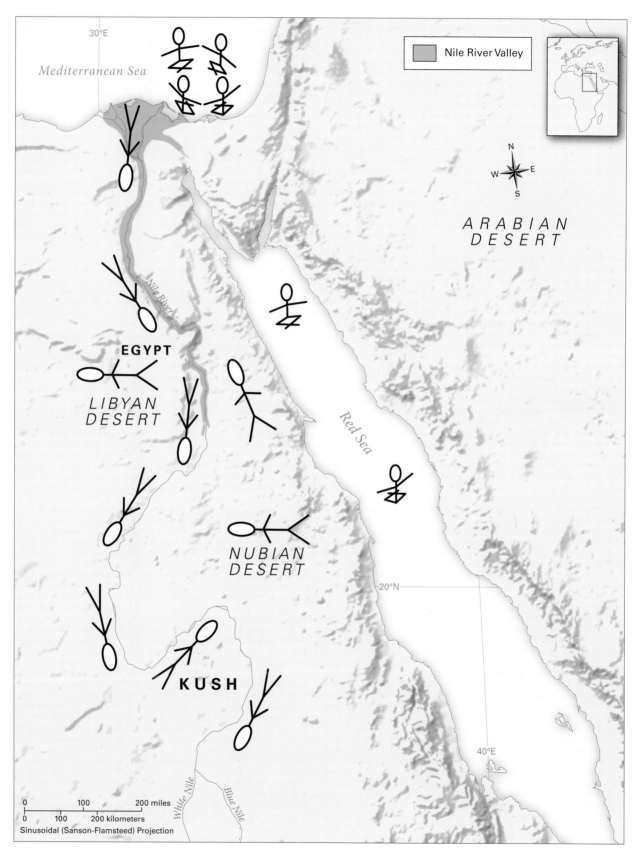

Nile River Valley

Mediterranean Sea

30°E

ARABIAN
DESERT

Nile River

EGYPT

LIBYAN
DESERT

Red Sea

NUBIAN
DESERT

20°N

KUSH

40°E

White Nile

Blue Nile

0   100   200 miles
0   100   200 kilometers
Sinusoidal (Sanson-Flamsteed) Projection

Physical Features of Canaan

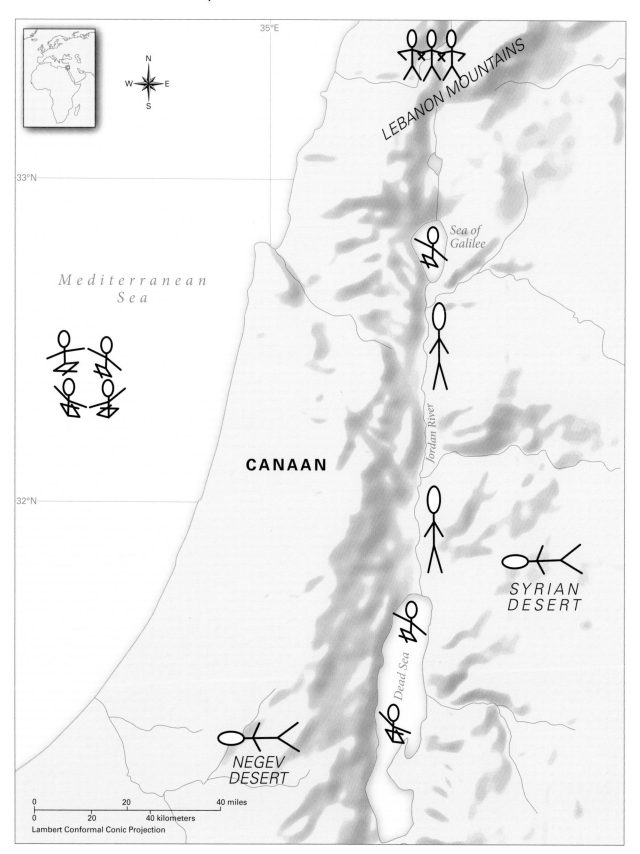

35°E

33°N

32°N

N
W   E
S

Mediterranean Sea

LEBANON MOUNTAINS

Sea of Galilee

Jordan River

CANAAN

Dead Sea

SYRIAN DESERT

NEGEV DESERT

0   20   40 miles
0   20   40 kilometers
Lambert Conformal Conic Projection

Postcard of Mount Rushmore

1. What interesting details do you see in the image on this postcard?

2. In whose honor do you think this monument was built?

3. Why do you think this monument was built to honor these four men?

4. What other monuments do you know that have been built to honor a person or group of people? Where are these monuments? Whom do they honor?

Our Tour Guide

The Great Pyramid at Giza

The White Chapel at Karnak

Hatshepsut's Temple at Dayr al-Bahri

Carving from Hatshepsut's Temple

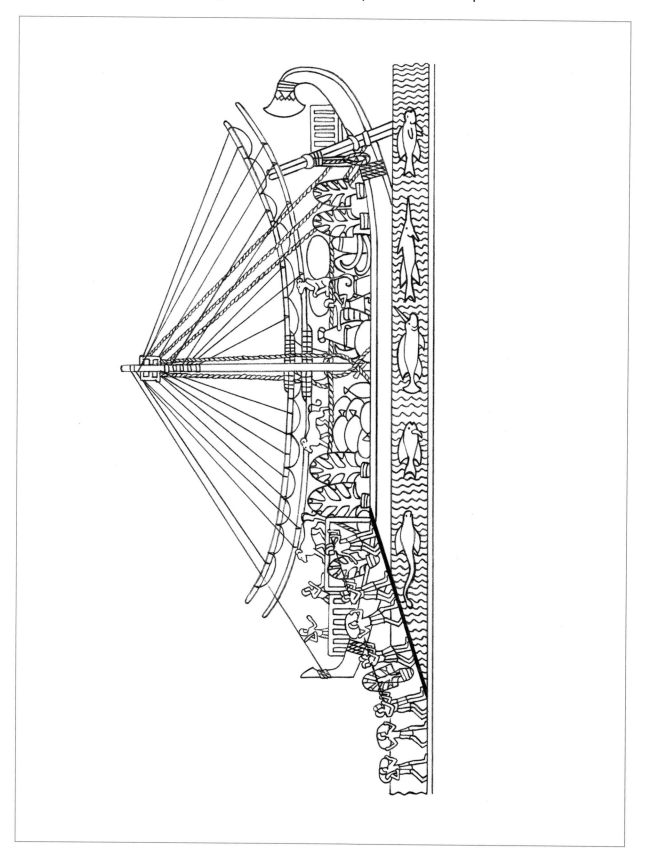

The Great Temple of Ramses II at Abu Simbel

Government Officials

Priests

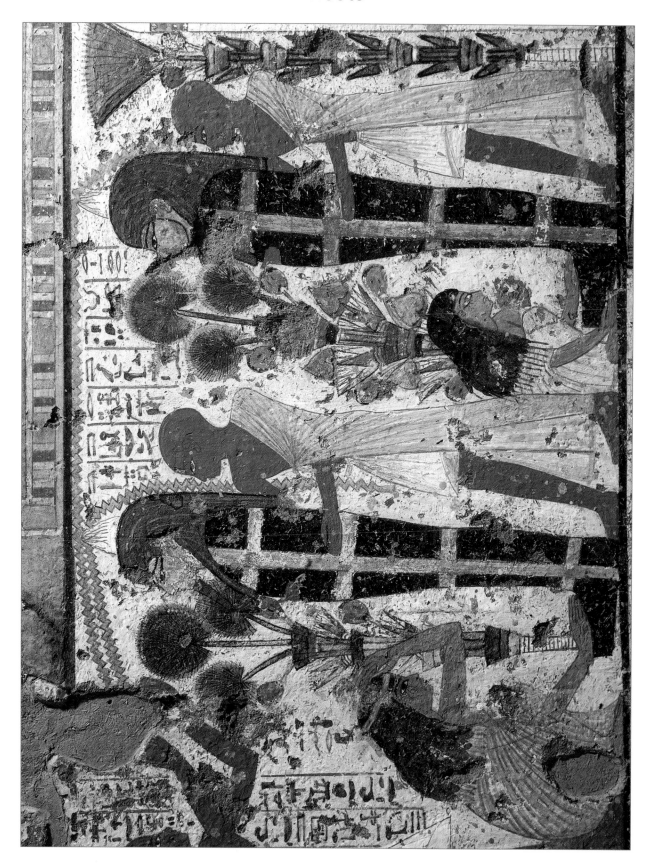

Scribes

Artisans

Peasants

Kushites Bringing Tribute to Egyptian Governor

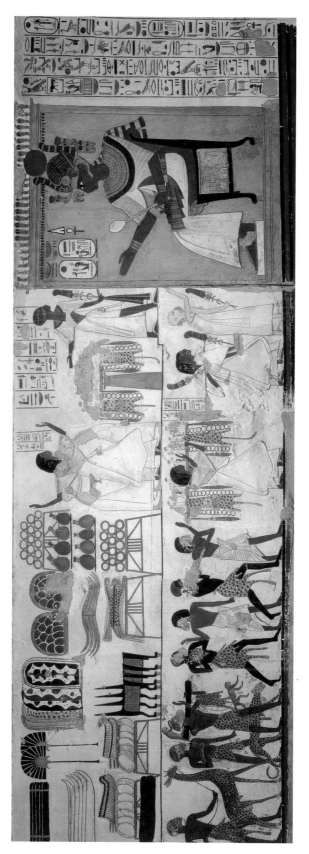

King Piye Receiving Gifts from Egyptian Princes

Kushite Ironworkers

Kandake Amanirenas and Prince Akinidad

Brahmaputra River

Deccan Plateau

Eastern and Western Ghats

Ganges River

Present-day India

Ganges River

Arabian Sea

Bay of Bengal

INDIAN OCEAN

Himalaya Mountains

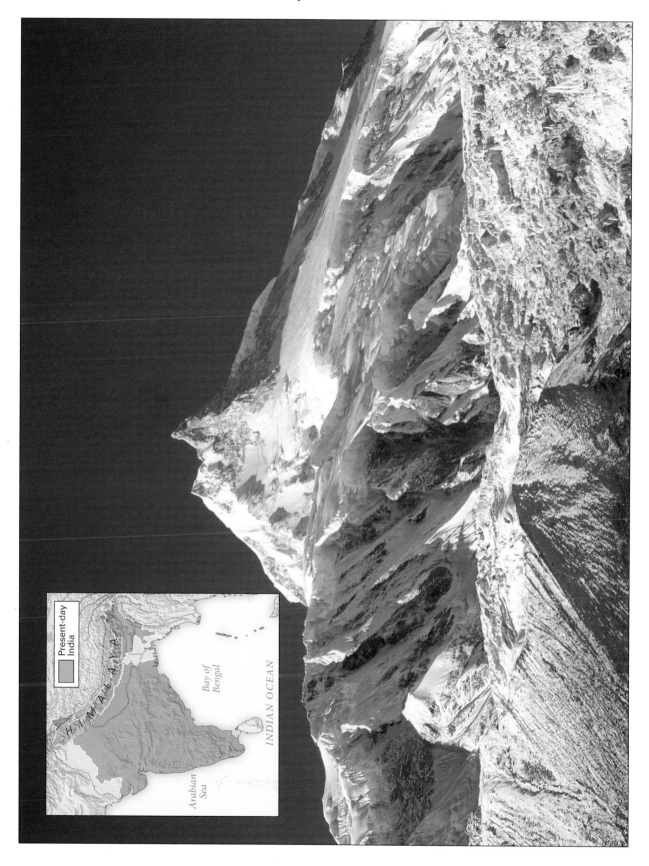

Present-day India

HIMALAYA

Bay of Bengal

INDIAN OCEAN

Arabian Sea

Hindu Kush

Present-day India

HINDU KUSH

Arabian Sea

Bay of Bengal

INDIAN OCEAN

Indus River

Thar Desert

Geographic Influence on Early Settlements in India

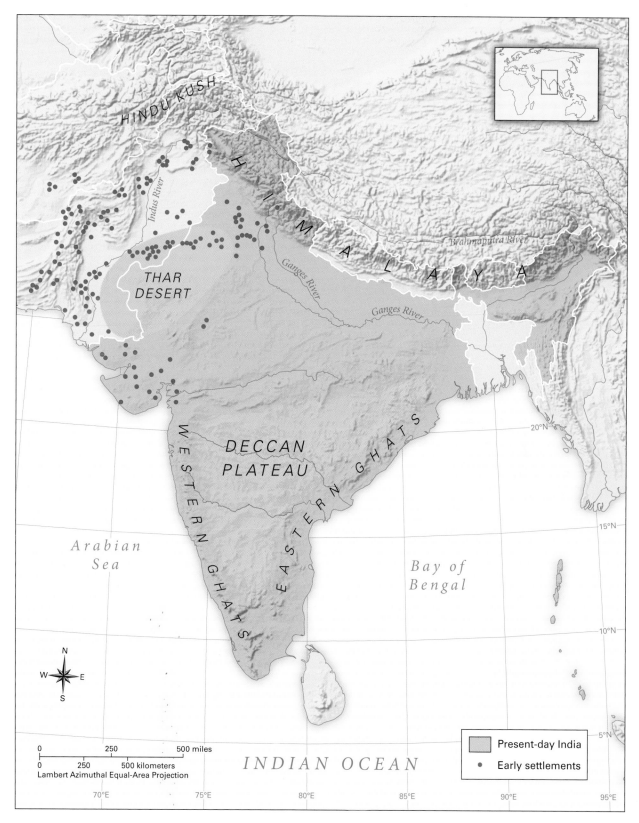

Ancient Indian Artifact

The Citadel at Mohenjodaro

Hindu Deities

Dharma

Karma

Samsara

Critical Thinking Question

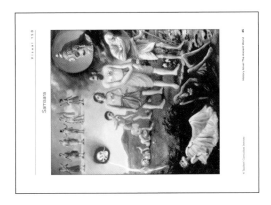

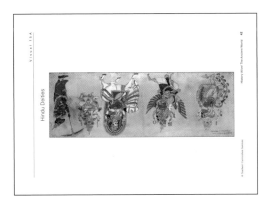

Use the information from your Reading Notes and from the images to answer the Critical Thinking Question below.

Critical Thinking Question: Which of these four Hindu beliefs do you think has most influenced life in India? Be prepared to share at least three reasons to support your response.

Siddhartha as a Baby

Siddhartha's Princely Life

Siddhartha Discovers Suffering

Siddhartha Becomes an Ascetic

Siddhartha Becomes the Buddha

Chinese Scroll

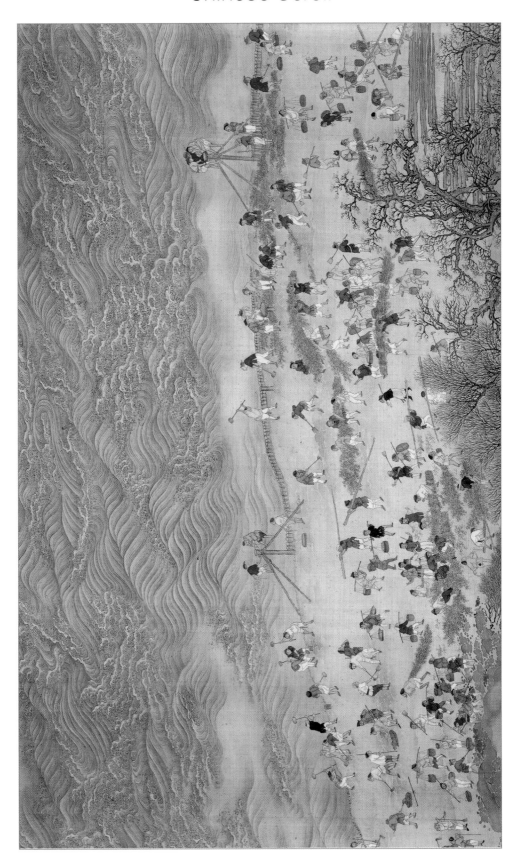

A Shang Tomb

Zhou Soldiers Destroying Peasants' Crops

Creating an Empire

Very Effective

How effectively did Qin Shihuangdi build an empire?

Very Ineffective

Standardizing the Culture

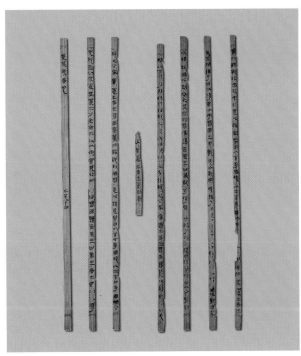

How effectively did Qin Shihuangdi unify China's culture?

Very Ineffective

Very Effective

Protecting the Northern Border

How effectively did Qin Shihuangdi protect China's borders?

Very Ineffective   **Very Effective**

Ending Opposition

How effectively did Qin Shihuangdi end opposition?

Very Ineffective

Very Effective

Warfare

1. In addition to scaring away enemies, how else did the kite help the Han army?

   A. It was used to send messages.
   B. It was used to deliver supplies.
   C. It provided light during night attacks.

Government

2. Who did the Han dynasty choose as government officials?

   A. those who wrote the best poems

   B. those who were already teachers

   C. those who scored well on exams

Agriculture

3. How did wheelbarrows help Han farmers?

   A. They made watering crops easier.

   B. They let farmers to plant more land.

   C. They helped farmers move products.

Industry

4. How did the deep-digging drill increase the Hans' supply of salt?

   A. got salt water from deep in the ground
   B. dug pits to get salt from seawater
   C. made storage bins to keep salt dry

Art

5. Which of the following Han inventions helps artists and scholars?

   A. paper
   B. carpets
   C. paintbrushes

Medicine

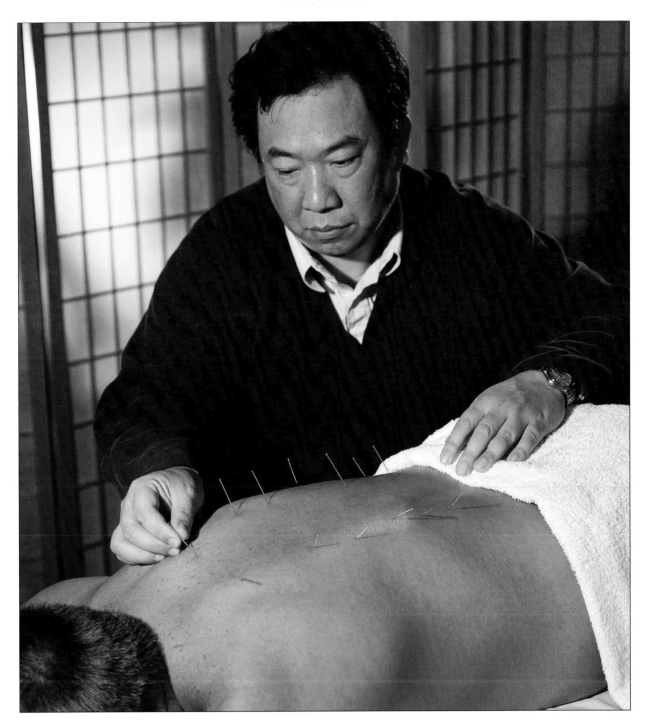

6. Why would a Chinese doctor stick needles into a person's body?

   A. to release evil spirits

   B. to punish bad people

   C. to balance yin and yang

Science

7. What could the Han learn from the earthquake device they invented?

   A. the depth of an earthquake

   B. the direction of an earthquake

   C. the damage caused by an earthquake

The Silk Road

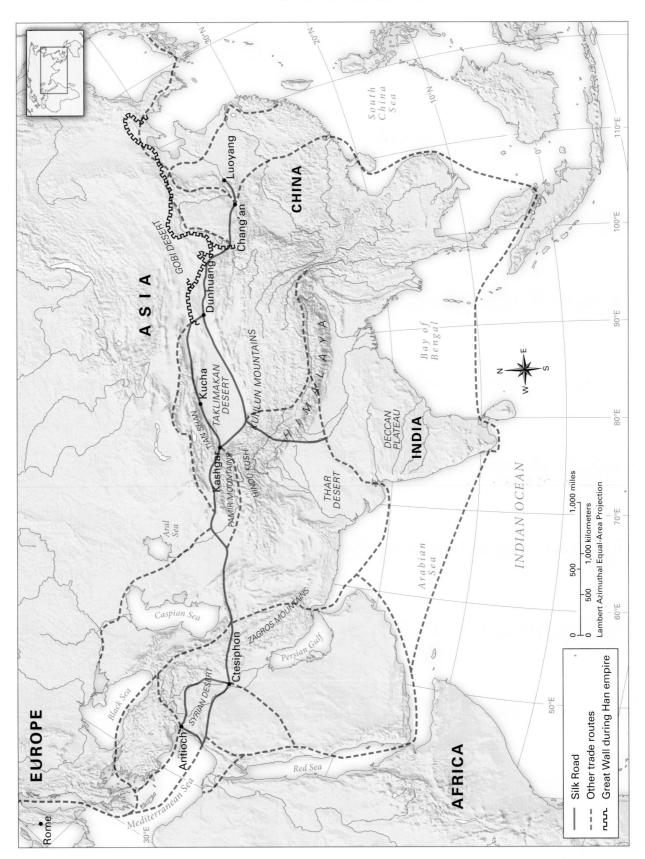

Physical Features of the Greek Peninsula

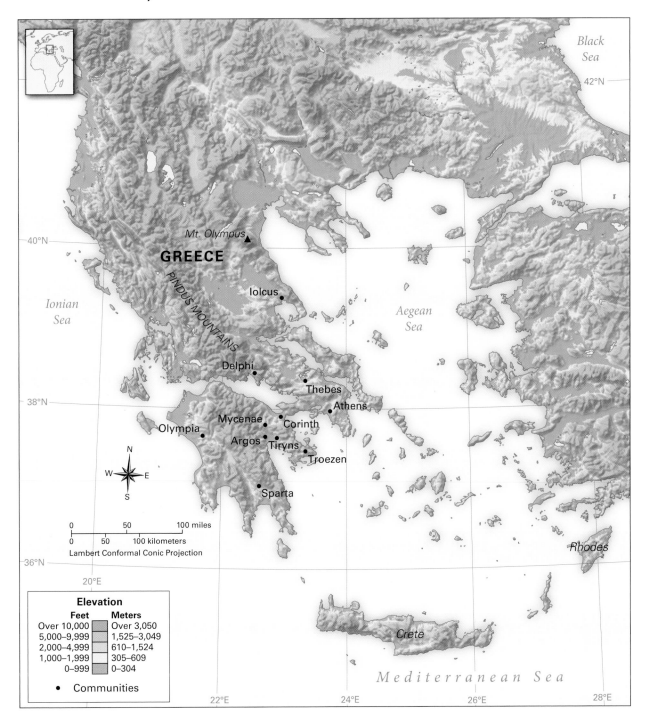

Physical Geography of Greece

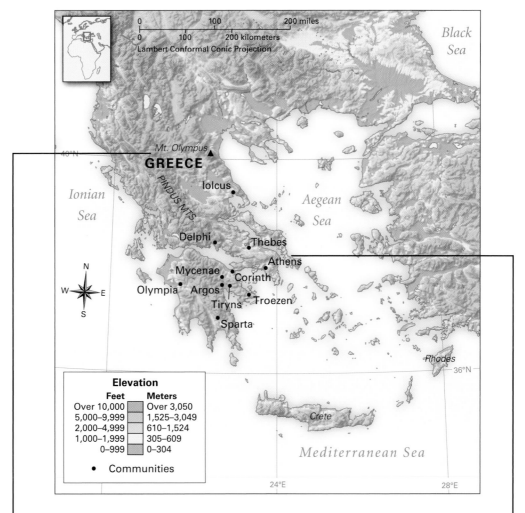

Black Sea

0   100   200 miles
0   100   200 kilometers
Lambert Conformal Conic Projection

Ionian Sea

40°N

Mt. Olympus ▲

GREECE

PINDUS MTS.

Iolcus •

Aegean Sea

Delphi •

• Thebes

• Athens

Mycenae •
• Corinth
Olympia •   Argos •
• Troezen
Tiryns •
• Sparta

Rhodes
36°N

Elevation

Feet		Meters
Over 10,000		Over 3,050
5,000–9,999		1,525–3,049
2,000–4,999		610–1,524
1,000–1,999		305–609
0–999		0–304

• Communities

Crete

Mediterranean Sea

24°E   28°E

The Mountains
Average Annual Temperature: 65°F
Average Monthly Precipitation: 3.5″

The Coast
Average Annual Temperature: 72°F
Average Monthly Precipitation: 1.4″

Ancient Greek Colonies and Trade Routes

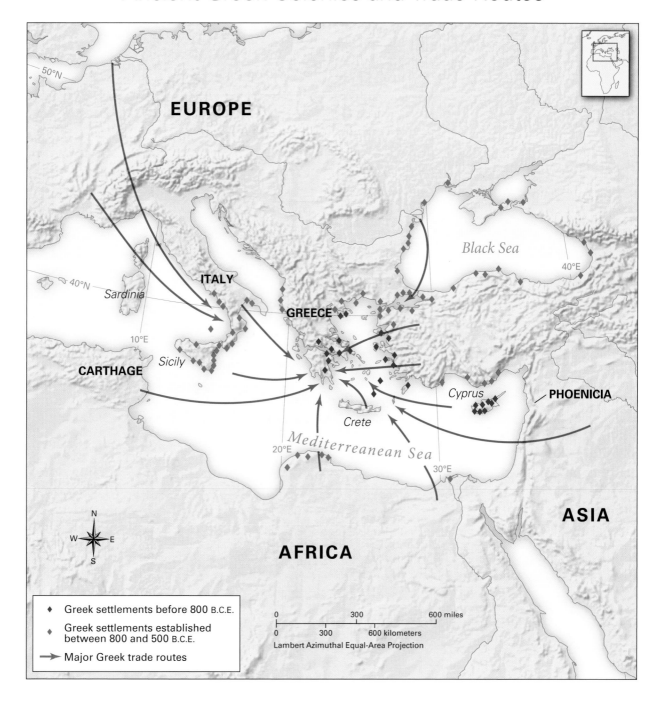

EUROPE

50°N

Black Sea

40°E

40°N

Sardinia

ITALY

GREECE

10°E

CARTHAGE

Sicily

Cyprus

PHOENICIA

Crete

Mediterreanean Sea

20°E

30°E

ASIA

AFRICA

N
W   E
S

♦   Greek settlements before 800 B.C.E.

♦   Greek settlements established between 800 and 500 B.C.E.

→   Major Greek trade routes

0   300   600 miles
0   300   600 kilometers
Lambert Azimuthal Equal-Area Projection

Athens and Sparta

Details of a Greek Temple

Metopes

Battle of Marathon

Battle of Thermopylae

Battle of Salamis

Battle of Plataea

Critical Thinking Question

The Persian Wars

40°N

Hellespont

Aegean
Sea

ASIA
MINOR

Thermopylae
480 B.C.E.

Delphi

Marathon
490 B.C.E.

IONIA

Plataea
479 B.C.E.

38°N

Athens

Olympia

Salamis
480 B.C.E.

Ionian
Sea

Sparta

N
W—E
S

36°N

20°E   22°E

24°E

Crete

	Persian Empire
	Greek states allied against Persia
	Neutral Greek states
✳	Greek victory
✸	Persian victory

0   50   100 miles
0   50   100 kilometers
Lambert Conformal Conic Projection

Mediterranean Sea

26°E   28°E

Use the information from the map and from your Reading
Notes to answer the Critical Thinking Question.

Critical Thinking Question
*Which of these factors best explains why the Greeks won
the Persian wars?*

A. The Greeks were joined together as allies.
B. The Greeks had better fighting equipment.
C. The Greeks knew the geography of the area.
D. The Greeks used clever military strategy.

Spreading Greek Ideas

Critical Thinking Question A Alexander planned to spread Greek culture and ideas to the people he had conquered. How successful was this part of his plan for uniting the empire?

Step 1: Discuss these questions with your group.

1. Why do you think Alexander insisted that government officials and soldiers speak only Greek? Was this a good or bad idea? Why?

2. How do you think non-Greeks felt about the Greeks when they saw Greek influences in the cities Alexander founded? Do you think it gave them more respect or less respect for the Greeks? Why?

Step 2: Individually, consider Critical Thinking Question A.

Rate this part of Alexander's plan for uniting the empire. Place your token on your group's spectrum to show your rating. Be prepared to share with your group at least two reasons that support your rating.

Very Unsuccessful   Very Successful

Step 3: As a group, discuss Critical Thinking Question A.

Have each group member share several reasons for his or her placement of the token on the spectrum. Then, as a group, determine where on the spectrum to rate this part of Alexander's plan. Choose a Presenter who is prepared to share your group's rating and reasons with the class.

Using Religion

Critical Thinking Question B Alexander planned to use religion to encourage people to accept him as their leader. How successful was this part of his plan for uniting the empire?

Step 1: Discuss these questions with your group.

1. If people believed that Alexander was a god, how might they have felt about his actions as a leader?
2. If people did not think that Alexander was a god, how might they have felt when he declared himself a god?

Step 2: Individually, consider Critical Thinking Question A.
Rate this part of Alexander's plan for uniting the empire. Place your token on your group's spectrum to show your rating. Be prepared to share with your group at least two reasons that support your rating.

Very Unsuccessful   Very Successful

Step 3: As a group, discuss Critical Thinking Question B.
Have each group member share several reasons for his or her placement of the token on the spectrum. Then, as a group, determine where on the spectrum to rate this part of Alexander's plan. Choose a Presenter who is prepared to share your group's rating and reasons with the class.

Adopting the Ways of Conquered Cultures

Critical Thinking Question C Alexander planned to adopt the cultural practices of the people he had conquered. How successful was this part of his plan for uniting the empire?

Step 1: Discuss these questions with your group.

1. Why do you think Alexander wore Persian-style clothing? Was this a good or bad idea? Why?
2. Why do you think Alexander encouraged marriage between Macedonians and Persians? Was this a good or bad idea? Why?

Step 2: Individually, consider Critical Thinking Question C.
Rate this part of Alexander's plan for uniting the empire. Place your token on your group's spectrum to show your rating. Be prepared to share with your group at least two reasons that support your rating.

Very Unsuccessful   Very Successful

Step 3: As a group, discuss Critical Thinking Question C.
Have each group member share several reasons for his or her placement of the token on the spectrum. Then, as a group, determine where on the spectrum to rate this part of Alexander's plan. Choose a Presenter who is prepared to share your group's rating and reasons with the class.

Medallion

Artistic Renditions of Ancient Greece and Rome

Scene from Ancient Greece

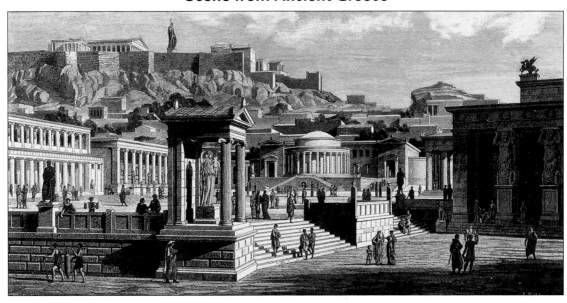

Scene from Ancient Rome

The Granger Collection, New York

Roman Street Scene

The Circus Maximus

The Roman Forum

Roman Mosaic

Detail of Trajan's Column

Street Scene in the Roman Empire

Jesus Teaching on a Mountainside

Christian Baptism

Christian Worship

Palm Sunday Procession